When the Soul Cries

By

Dottie Randazzo

When the Soul Cries

by

Dottie Randazzo

Published by:

Creative Dreaming

6433 Topanga Cyn. Blvd.

Woodland Hills, CA 91303

All rights reserved. No part of this book may be reproduced or transmitted in any form or by any means, electronic or mechanical, including photocopying, recording or by any information storage and retrieval system, without permission from the author, except for the inclusion of brief quotations in a review.

Copyright © 2008 by Dottie Randazzo

ISBN 978-0-6151-8654-2

By Dottie Randazzo

Praying 101 for Spiritual Enlightenment
Praying 101 for Men
Praying 101 for Women
Praying 101 for Kids & Teens
Praying 101 for Parents

The Feeling
Trust
Are you a Spiritual Hypochondriac?
Gardening at Night

Fiction
The Blue Girl

What does it mean
when your soul cries?

Would you know if this were happening to you?

Are you aware of the function of your soul?

Could you identify your soul?

Dictionary.com identifies your soul as:

- The principle of life, feeling, thought and action in humans, regarded as a distinct entity separate from the body, and commonly held to be separable in existence from the body; the spiritual part of humans as distinct from the physical part.

- The spiritual part of humans regarded in its moral aspect, or as believed to survive death and be subject to happiness or misery in a life to come.

- The disembodied spirit of a deceased person.

- The emotional part of human nature; the seat of the feelings or sentiments.

- A human being; person.

- *Christian Science.* God; the divine source of all identity and individuality.

Any thought, desire or deed creates etheric energy that marks your soul.

The purpose of your soul is to grow and transform.

Each soul comes with
the freedom of choice
and purpose.

The expression of this purpose is vital for your soul to evolve.

Your soul must have experiences in order to evolve.

A very young child can hear its soul's calling.

As the child grows up, external influences, such as parents and the media, fill the child's head, therefore, pushing away the soul's agenda.

Wanting to be loved and accepted, the child then begins a journey that is not in accordance with the soul's agenda.

Here is where conflict arises and life gets difficult.

The individual is doing so much thinking that it can't *feel* what the soul desires.

The urge to be accepted and fit in with the masses becomes more important than honoring your true desire.

You think your accomplishments will bring approval and recognition.

Some know what they *feel* they should be doing; however, they put it off until later in life when they have finished doing what they think they are suppose to do.

Sometimes a soul's calling is so loud that an individual can hear it and *feel* it, several times a day, for years, but continues to ignore it.

This is when the soul begins to cry.

This is when self-sabotaging behavior comes into play.

This is when things begin to happen in a person's life that causes pain, misery and grief.

Imagine if you had a bird and everyone around you began to tell you to feed your bird cooked navy beans. Your bird doesn't like cooked navy beans, but in an effort not to starve, however, he eats the beans. The bird becomes very unhappy, gets sick, and eventually dies.

Similarly, you are not feeding, nurturing, nourishing, or being kind to your soul when you live your life the way you think or are told it should be lived instead of the way you truly *feel* it should be lived.

Why would someone not live the life they were meant to live?

Peer pressure from parents could be a reason.

Your parents want you to have a better life than they had, so they put you on a road that they think is best for you.

Acceptance by others
is another reason.

The desire to fit in and
be accepted is fueled
by ego and insecurities.

Of course, as a teenager it is difficult to recognize the reasons behind the behavior.

The choices that one makes can be to please another, such as parents and friends, all in an effort to garner acceptance, approval and love, or fill the desire to fit in.

When the ego and
insecurities are at play,
one cannot hear the
soul's true desires.

An individual may marry or be in a relationship that they think is best for them merely because it wins the approval of friends and/or family.

An individual may study and hold jobs that they think are best for them, once again, while seeking approval from friends, family or even their communities.

How would you know
if you are following
your soul's calling?

Ask yourself this question, "How does it *feel*?" Forget about your parents, your friends and/or your associates.

I know it is hard.

Up until this moment,
you have basically
lived your life for
them.

To make this easier for yourself, imagine you have just been beamed up to Jupiter.

You are the only one there. No one can hear what you say, think, or *feel*. And by the way, whatever happens on Jupiter stays on Jupiter.

So how do you *feel* about your choices?

Do you *feel* you have chosen exactly what you desire?

Were your choices influenced by someone else or something else?

Ignore those thoughts such as, "Your parents wanted the best for you and that's why they put you on this road; they really, really cared."

I am not saying your parents didn't love or care for you, or even have your best interest at heart.

They were merely unaware that when you were born, your soul had an agenda.

Your soul has a unique gift that should be creatively expressed.

So your parents acted the way they thought parents should act.

It wasn't malicious and they should be forgiven.

Occupations and relationships are the major sources of soul suffering.

Do you *feel* that the relationship you are in is the best one for you?

Do you *feel* it is one that allows you the freedom to grow and follow your dreams?

Is it supportive of your choices?

Would you be allowed to go and live in the rainforest for six months if that is what you desired?

Would you have to make sure that your desires are in accordance with your partner's desires in order to be accomplished?

If you pursued your desires, would it affect your relationship?

Would your partner *feel* unloved or abandoned if you took off to the rainforest?

Would your partner try to talk you out of it, or would they be supportive and offer assistance in fulfilling your desires?

True, deep, meaningful love never dies and never goes away, even when you do.

When you have loved
another with the purest
intention, your soul has
a branded mark on it
that stays forever, even
into other lifetimes.

Some souls go through a lifetime never acquiring a brand of love.

Some souls obtain a branding of love only once during a lifetime because the individual thinks this is enough.

This individual will push away any love that tries to enter their life. Hence, they are on a road with many conflicts.

Some souls are branded with love by many in a lifetime.

Love will come into a lifetime many times.

A soul's purpose is to love, be loved, and creatively express love.

A soul is not happy
when they are not
loving another or
accepting the love of
another.

Nothing a soul will ever experience will compare to the *feeling* of love.

Where there is no love,
there is instead
negativity and conflict.

So while you are here on Jupiter, it is time to do some soul searching.

Ask yourself, "Who am I?"

Forget about your
parents, your
education, your career
and your relationships.

They aren't here on Jupiter and they don't define YOU.

That's the illusion many buy into, that they are everything that is external. They are their jobs, their families, their cars and jewelry. It's stuff; it's not you.

So here you are sitting on a rock on Jupiter, no job, no family, no car and no friends.

Who are you?

Sit with a pad and pen
and write,
"Who am I?"

This is soul searching
at its finest.

You are not allowed to write anything that is external. For example, I am a CEO, I am a father, and I am a husband.

Those are not who you are. Those are titles.

OK, chances are you can't come up with a thing to write.

Don't *feel* bad – you are joined by many.

It takes great effort to block out all the useless chatter to hear your own voice, the voice of your soul.

Let's say you can hear
your soul's cry.

You have these urges and desires.

They seem so foreign
and you aren't sure
how to make them
happen.

Chances are this is why you have dismissed them, because you can't see the road ahead. You can't see the outcome. So you don't even venture down the road.

Because you cannot predict the success of a writing career, you stay in a safe and what you think is a predictable job. I understand the need for an income to provide a roof over your head.

So instead of quitting your job cold turkey, because that would certainly be real scary, what if you were to spend all of your free time pursuing the writing that your soul desired?

The entire time, focusing on your creative intent and not the outcome.

Imagine spending your non-accounting time feeding your soul, doing exactly what you desired.

Are you in a relationship that isn't working for you?

Chances are it never really worked from the get go.

But to be a good sport,
you went along with it.

You think you can't leave.

What about the children, what about your spouse that is still in love with you?

How do you think your children and spouse are being affected by your *feelings*, not your actions?

You are *feeling* you don't want to be there, but your actions are different, because you keep showing up.

Hello – do you smell drama and conflict brewing?

You probably argue over the silliest things because you just don't want to be in that situation anymore.

Does that sound fair to you?

Does that sound fair to your children?

Does that sound fair to your spouse?

Did you know that you can love someone and not have to live under the same roof with them? Go figure.

Does leaving a situation in which you no longer *feel* is right for you necessarily mean you no longer love those who are important?

If you really loved them, wouldn't you tell them how you *feel*?

Are you afraid of hurting them?

Are you sure you aren't hurting them now?

Are you sure by pretending and not expressing yourself that they aren't suffering?

If they really loved you, would they want you to stay in a situation that you really didn't want to be in?

Is the argument that they are giving you fueled by love, anger, ego and/or insecurity?

Most stay in relationships for fear of being alone.

What a sad way to live
your life.

If you don't enjoy your own company, then how do you expect anyone else to?

Most relationship arguments are over two things – "How much do you love me?" and "Who is in charge?"

Can you just be loved without being measured and does anyone have to be in charge?

Everything in life changes and yet many are so naive to think that their relationships will not change.

Relationships, like your soul, need the freedom to grow and transform and experience.

I am not promoting free love and open relationships. However, if a couple chooses this lifestyle and it works for them, then so be it.

You can make a commitment to someone and roam around the planet freely, without a ball and chain, knowing that you can be trusted to uphold your commitment.

If you made a commitment and you *feel* it is no longer working for you or you have outgrown it, you can talk about it and come up with an arrangement that you *feel* comfortable with.

You can commit to being honest and trustworthy as long as it *feels* like the right thing to do.

I know this doesn't sound at all romantic or fairy tale-ish.

Can you make a commitment to someone without the words of a traditional marriage?

Why does the commitment have to be "Till death do us part"?

You don't commit to anything in life till death.

And yet, two growing, evolving souls make an unreasonable, unattainable commitment.

If they do manage to stay together for a lifetime in honor of that commitment, rarely is there love.

Resentment is usually the case because at least one soul has been sacrificed, if not both, by the mere act of an unreasonable commitment.

The words of a marriage vow make it scarier to break.

After all, they are taken, "In the eyes of God."

Well, if you actually believe this, then I want to know why you act as if those same eyes of God, that watched you make a marriage vow, are not watching you every day?

What about a real commitment, one that offers accountability?

How about saying,

"I commit to always be honest with you about my *feelings* and intentions.

I commit to this relationship as long as it is healthy for both of us.

I commit that I shall show you love, compassion and trust.

I commit that I will do whatever I can to empower and support you in your life journey.

I commit that I will act responsible in my actions, thoughts and desires.

Should I fail to live up to my commitment, I give you my blessings to jump ship and create a better life for yourself."

Doesn't that sound more real?

Doesn't it sound like
the truth?

It has been said that the truth hurts.

It actually doesn't hurt the one who is telling it.

The truth only hurts the one who is hearing it when their ego and insecurities are being attacked.

If their egos or insecurities were not affected, they would experience no pain.

The truth would show
love, compassion,
caring and
understanding.

In order to act in the best interest of your soul, you must tell the truth.

How do your choices
affect your soul?

Your soul's evolution is
based on the principal
of cause and effect.

The way in which you handle life's challenges will directly affect the evolution of your soul.

Read that sentence again.

Note, it is not the challenges that affect your soul, but the way in which you deal with the challenges.

Each lifetime is one of nearly limitless opportunities and possibilities.

Instead of letting our life unfold by following our soul's desire, we put restrictions and blinders on ourselves.

Most wind up living a life of routine, void of choices and possibilities.

If you are still sitting here on Jupiter, I want to give you something to ponder.

How much are you an active participant in your life?

Are you just going for the ride?

Are you just living the life you were handed?

I hate to be the one who tells you, but no one handed out lives already scripted, and there really isn't an Easter Bunny!

If you were handed a life already scripted, then why would you have been given free will?

Don't you think there would have been a conflict of interest?

Do you really, honestly, I mean really, think you were given the ability to make choices and at the same time given a life that was already planned?

Did you even know that your soul has a purpose?

If you didn't know this,
then you are not aware
of what the purpose is.

Did you know that every experience you have in this lifetime is for the sole purpose of your personal growth?

Did you know that your soul experiences the consequences of its previous choices – just as you, in your everyday life, experience the consequences of your actions?

Bet you didn't know that your soul can grow even when you have made the "wrong choice."

A lot can be learned from mistakes we have made.

It is far worse to not make a choice than to make a wrong one.

Just the act of choosing allows movement, growth and activity for your soul.

Your soul is unique because it comes with the gift of free will.

This free will offers the
amazing opportunity
for your soul to grow
and evolve.

Are you exercising your free will in your life?

When you aren't exercising your free will and going against your better judgment, your soul will cry.

Equally as important as your actions to your soul's evolution are your thoughts and intentions.

Thinking positive thoughts and exercising positive intentions aids in your soul's evolution.

Every thought, choice or decision you make is made with the exercised free will of your soul.

Some choices may lead you down a path of happiness and bliss, while other choices may lead you down a path of problems and conflicts.

When you become aware of the fact that every experience that pops up in your life is good or bad and assists you in the evolution of your soul, then and only then can the events and circumstances become meaningful and purposeful.

Two people can experience the same event. It is how the individuals handle the event that will determine the next event.

If your house burns down, you can go down the road of loss and grief, or you can go down the road of change and opportunity.

The choice is exercised
by your free will.

The choice may or may not assist in your soul's evolution.

The soul's evolution is exercised by free will.

Free will comes in two forms – good and bad.

So what if you exercise your free will in a negative way, will your soul evolve?

Your soul will cry and your soul will suffer.

You will experience many painful situations where you will have choices to exercise your free will.

Should you choose negatively, you will encounter negative situations to deal with.

Drama fuels drama.

Conflict fuels conflict.

If your intent is to help another human being, your soul will evolve and you will experience happiness.

If your intent is merely for personal gain, your soul will suffer and you will experience conflicts.

Look at the opportunities you have in front of you every single day.

These are wonderful
opportunities for you.

The good, the bad, the fun, the not-so-fun, the pleasant person, the grumpy person, all are opportunities for the evolution of your soul.

Just as everything you encounter affects your soul, your actions, your intent and your thoughts provide the opportunity for another's soul to evolve.

With the awareness of free will comes the awareness of responsibility.

If you are aware, you must be responsible.

If you run over
someone with your car,
you are responsible.

The mere fact that you did not see them does not in any way make you unaccountable for your actions.

You won't hop on the Yellow Brick Road of figuring out your life until you can answer the question, "Who am I?"

If you have come as far as answering that question, then next you should ask yourself if your actions are in accordance with who you really are?

If your actions are not in accordance with who you really are, well, your soul may be crying.

If you are reading this book, you are a spiritual person.

When faced with the fear of being yourself, of pursuing your soul's agenda, remember that God and/or the universe has always and will always provide what you need, when you need it.

Even the bad stuff is there for you to learn and grow from.

Everything in life happens for your own best interest.

Every living thing has a purpose.

The purpose is to be what you are supposed to be.

A seed's purpose is to bloom into a flower. A dog's purpose is to be a dog.

Your purpose is to be you.

Have you forgotten
how to be you?

A seed doesn't forget it is supposed to bloom into a flower. A dog doesn't forget how to be a dog.

Only people forget
how to be themselves.

Remember, you are not anything external.

You are not anything
that you can reach out
and touch.

You aren't your education, your house, your job or your parents.

If you have forgotten who you are, it might be helpful to spend a few minutes, every chance you get, to ask yourself some questions like:

What are my passions?

What are my
desires?

What is my purpose?

Am I exercising my free will in my life?

Who am I?

Exercising your free will is essential to living the life you desire.

The key to a happy, fulfilling life is to be truthful to yourself about yourself.

It is not important how others treat you. It is more important how you treat them.

If they treat you badly, remove them from your life. You don't have to be mean and hurtful to do this. How you do this is what really counts.

When you do not follow your soul's desire, you open up the opportunity for disease.

You create chaos
within your being.

So sit on Jupiter as long as you like and ask yourself as many times as you need to, "Who am I?"

You will know the
right answer when you
feel it.

www.ingramcontent.com/pod-product-compliance
Lightning Source LLC
Chambersburg PA
CBHW051751040426
42446CB00007B/312